THIS BOOK BELONGS TO

_____

- -

_____

SCHOLASTIC PANDA EDUCATION

ISBN: 978-1-953149-32-9

Copyright © 2022 by Scholastic Panda Education

Hello!

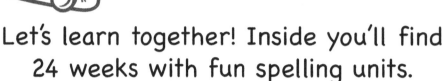

Let's learn together! Inside you'll find 24 weeks with fun spelling units.

Each unit will have 4 practice pages.

Remember to:

1. Look at each spelling word
2. Say the word out loud
3. Write the word
4. Color all the doodles
5. Have tons of fun!

Don't forget to check your spelling of each word after you've finished.

Did You Enjoy This Book?

Scholastic Panda Education

We'd love to hear your thoughts.

Leave this book a review and we'll send you something special.

We may even provide you with a digital copy of our next educational book.

DIGITAL ANSWER KEY

Found at the back of the book

SPELLING WORDS

Trace the word on the left,
then write it two more times on the right.

1. a
2. as
3. am
4. an
5. if
6. is
7. his
8. I
9. on
10. of

Write a spelling word in each turtle shell

Draw a line to connect the matching words

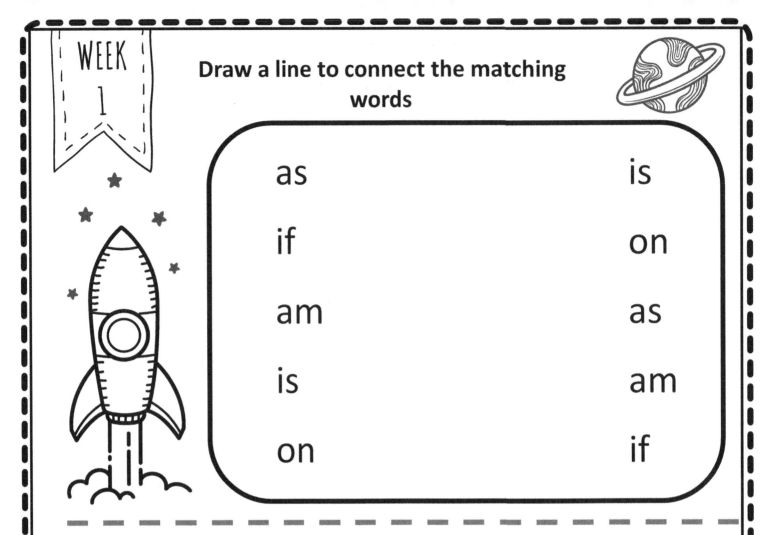

as	is
if	on
am	as
is	am
on	if

Put the following words in their correct shape boxes

of   an   his

Use a marker and highlight the spelling words below

dot	a	cup	as
yes	an	if	I
tell	am	his	so
is	no	now	is
up	hope	of	on

Use the words below to complete the sentences.

a   his

I   if

Can _____ go?

Is this _____ toy?

_____ you want it.

He loves _____ dog.

SPELLING WORDS

Trace the word on the left,
then write it two more times on the right.

1. us

2. up

3. me

4. he

5. she

6. we

7. be

8. so

9. no

10. go

Write a spelling word from your list in each of the balloons.

WEEK 2

Draw a line to connect the matching words

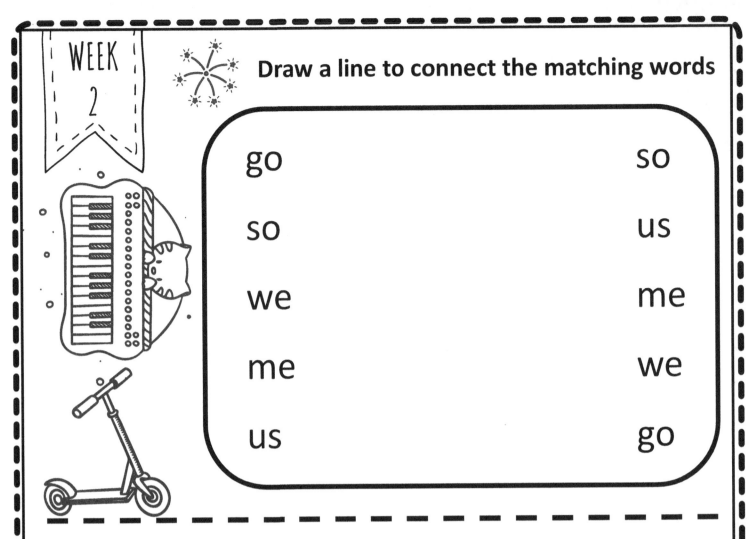

go	so
so	us
we	me
me	we
us	go

Put the following words in their correct shape boxes

be she no

Use a marker and highlight the spelling words below

too	box	boat	she
we	he	red	me
will	go	his	so
us	new	now	true
be	up	of	no

Use the words below to complete the sentences.

us
we
she
be

Come with _____ .

_____ likes them.

Please _____ safe.

_____ are happy.

SPELLING WORDS

1. at
2. bat
3. cat
4. fat
5. hat
6. mat
7. pat
8. rat
9. sat
10. flat

Trace the word on the left,
then write it two more times on the right.

Find each of the spelling words in the word search below

I	W	N	D	M	A	T	Q	I	N
O	V	I	M	E	K	R	A	H	X
W	O	T	D	D	A	T	F	D	D
H	D	E	M	R	A	Z	O	C	W
F	A	T	I	B	F	S	I	A	F
D	R	T	K	M	L	A	D	T	E
O	H	U	E	R	A	T	T	E	G
X	K	O	G	Y	T	A	B	S	G
X	G	K	N	F	P	Q	X	U	G
R	X	Y	M	X	M	E	Z	Q	D

AT

BAT

CAT

FAT

HAT

MAT

PAT

RAT

SAT

FLAT

Under each picture write the correct spelling of each word

_____

_____

_____

_____

Draw a line to connect the matching words

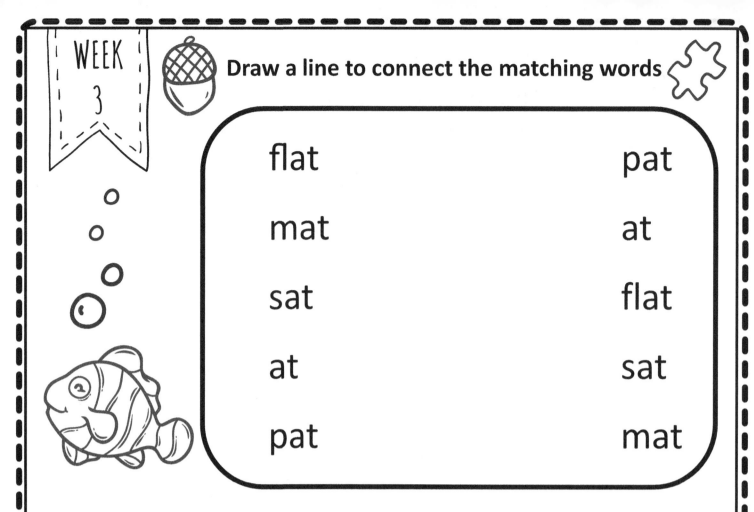

flat	pat
mat	at
sat	flat
at	sat
pat	mat

Put the following words in their correct shape boxes

bat   at   hat

Use a marker and highlight the spelling words below

red	how	if	him
you	bat	sip	sat
true	who	at	us
we	tree	tip	true
cat	up	of	mat

Use the words below to complete the sentences.

fat

sat

rat

flat

He _____ down.

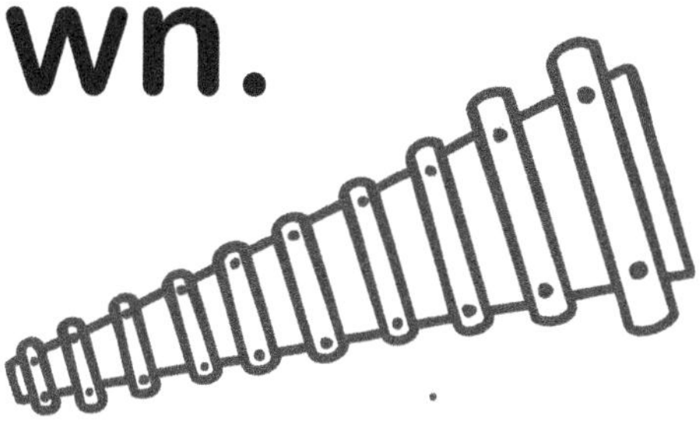

The _____ runs fast.

It is a _____ cat.

The road is _____ .

SPELLING WORDS

Trace the word on the left,
then write it two more times on the right.

1. that

2. the

3. they

4. them

5. then

6. this

7. you

8. your

9. my

10. by

Find each of the spelling words in the word search below

N	H	E	T	Y	T	H	T	E	T
H	Y	Y	N	T	T	A	E	E	T
E	H	S	S	N	E	Y	T	E	H
T	H	Y	S	U	H	M	A	E	E
T	H	I	N	T	E	T	E	U	Y
E	H	E	Y	H	T	T	H	U	M
T	H	E	M	O	H	R	O	E	S
T	H	A	T	Y	U	Y	E	H	M
R	E	E	B	O	M	Y	Y	N	Y
E	M	H	Y	E	T	O	O	Y	R

THAT

THE

THEY

THEM

THEN

THIS

YOU

YOUR

MY

BY

Choose four words from the spelling list and write them below. Color each letter of the word with a different color.

_____ _____

_____ _____

Draw a line to connect the matching words

that	this
they	they
your	that
this	the
the	your

Put the following words in their correct shape boxes

you   my   then

Use a crayon and circle the spelling words below

the   how   this   her

off   you   my   blue

dark   then   at   us

ox   that   them   true

by   up   they   your

Use the words below to complete the sentences.

WEEK 4

your   them

my   this

What is _____?

She is _____ mom.

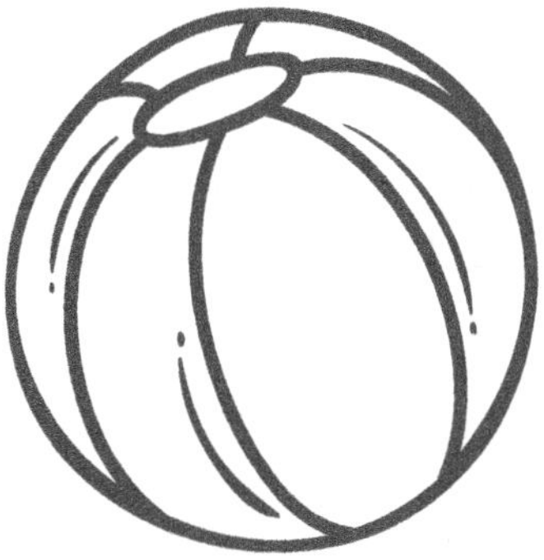

Is that _____ ball?

Wow, look at _____ run!

SPELLING WORDS

1. it
2. bit
3. fit
4. hit
5. lit
6. kit
7. spit
8. pit
9. its
10. sit

Trace the word on the left,
then write it two more times on the right.

WEEK 5

Find each of the spelling words in the word search below

ITS	
SPIT	
SIT	
PIT	
LIT	
KIT	
HIT	
FIT	
IT	
BIT	

T	F	T	T	S	T	I	I	S	I
I	I	T	T	F	T	I	K	F	I
S	I	T	P	K	S	I	T	T	T
H	P	B	I	I	I	I	I	B	H
S	F	I	T	S	T	I	T	T	I
H	I	T	T	I	T	T	I	S	I
S	I	I	T	S	T	T	S	T	I
K	L	T	I	I	I	S	K	I	T
T	F	P	I	T	P	I	T	I	T
H	T	B	S	H	P	S	T	I	T

Choose four words from the spelling list and write them below. Color each letter of the word with a different color.

_____   _____

_____   _____

Draw a line to connect the matching words

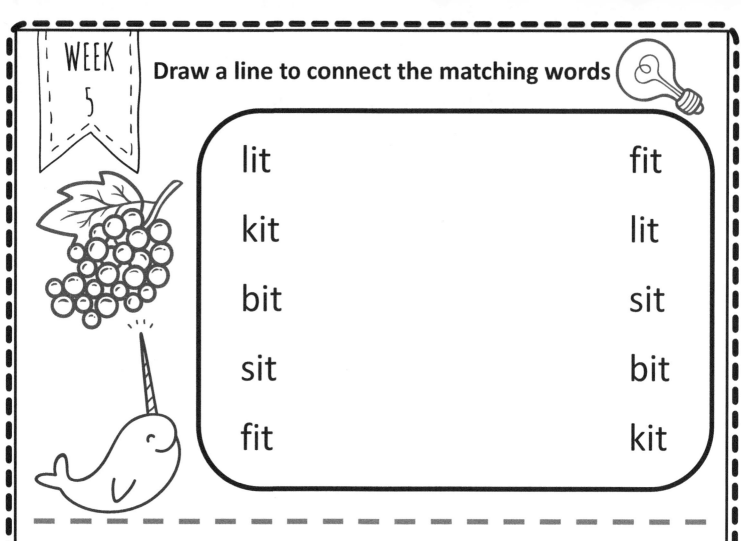

lit	fit
kit	lit
bit	sit
sit	bit
fit	kit

Put the following words in their correct shape boxes

hit   its   spit

Circle and connect the spelling words to help the bee get to the bottom

wow	it	fit	corn
fly	then	by	hit
sit	pit	lit	kit
spit	that	rug	sun
stop	its	bit	bee

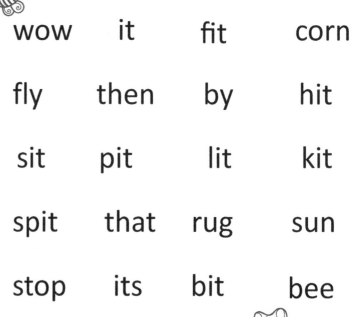

Use the words below to complete the sentences.

fit
kit
sit
lit

Does this shirt _____ me?

Please _____ still.

They _____ the fire.

That is a cool paint _____ !

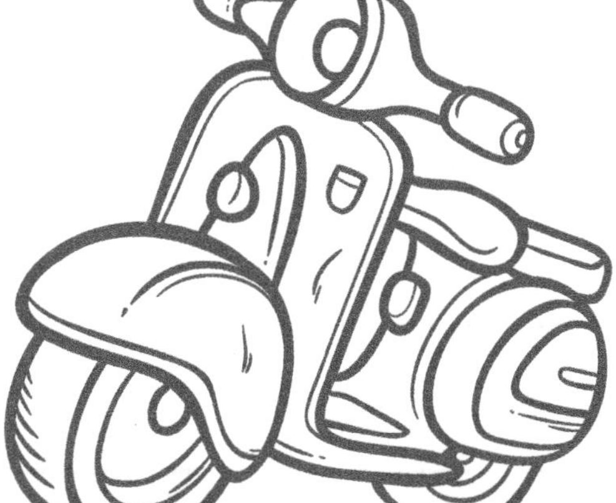

SPELLING WORDS

1. bet
2. get
3. jet
4. let
5. met
6. pet
7. net
8. wet
9. mom
10. set

Trace the word on the left,
then write it two more times on the right.

Find each of the spelling words in the word search below

MOM		Y	N	P	E	T	R	U	N	D	Y

MOM
WET
SET
PET
NET
MET
LET
JET
GET
BET

Y	N	P	E	T	R	U	N	D	Y
V	E	Q	E	T	C	S	H	B	G
U	T	W	B	E	T	P	X	E	G
Z	O	Q	Q	H	X	A	F	Y	D
D	O	P	S	O	T	Q	J	Y	E
M	O	M	X	E	K	L	E	S	J
W	N	Q	S	P	M	E	T	W	K
W	Q	R	T	B	K	T	X	R	H
Y	K	G	G	E	T	Z	Q	Q	P
X	A	V	Z	D	Y	X	A	J	X

Choose four words from the spelling list and write them below. Color each letter of the word with a different color.

_____   _____

_____   _____

Draw a line to connect the matching words

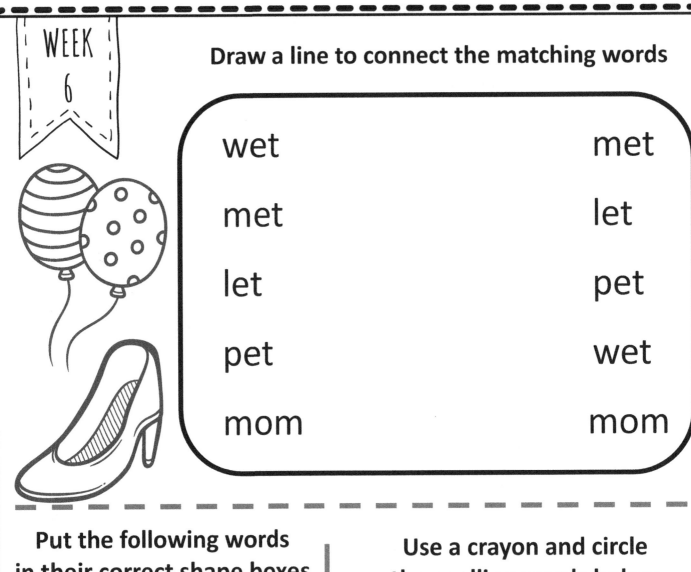

wet	met
met	let
let	pet
pet	wet
mom	mom

Put the following words in their correct shape boxes

jet   mom   set

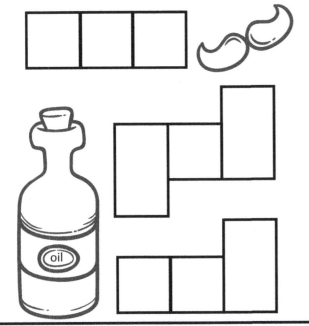

Use a crayon and circle the spelling words below

get	cow	swim	corn
fly	dot	net	green
rock	box	rug	met
bet	pet	jet	won
not	food	let	sun

Use the words below to complete the sentences.

let   mom   met   wet

I _____ a new friend.

Please _____ me in.

I love my _____ .

My socks are _____ !

SPELLING WORDS

1. dot
2. hot
3. lot
4. her
5. him
6. part
7. spot
8. slot
9. pot
10. not

Trace the word on the left,
then write it two more times on the right.

Find each of the spelling words in the word search below

HER		R	D	Q	L	W	X	W	H	B	P
DOT		G	Z	R	O	P	O	T	A	Y	S
HIM		I	K	K	T	N	I	Q	H	J	A
HOT		S	L	O	T	O	Z	S	U	R	M
PART		T	W	D	O	T	E	T	T	I	F
LOT		F	H	O	T	V	G	G	H	A	G
SPOT		U	H	E	C	L	L	E	A	F	R
NOT		Z	P	A	R	T	J	S	P	O	T
SLOT		X	A	Q	M	W	S	M	G	D	E
POT		J	Z	J	F	B	V	K	K	P	Q

Choose four words from the spelling list and write them below. Color each letter of the word with a different color.

_____   _____

_____   _____

WEEK 7

Write a different spelling word in each chalkboard below

Draw a line to connect the matching words

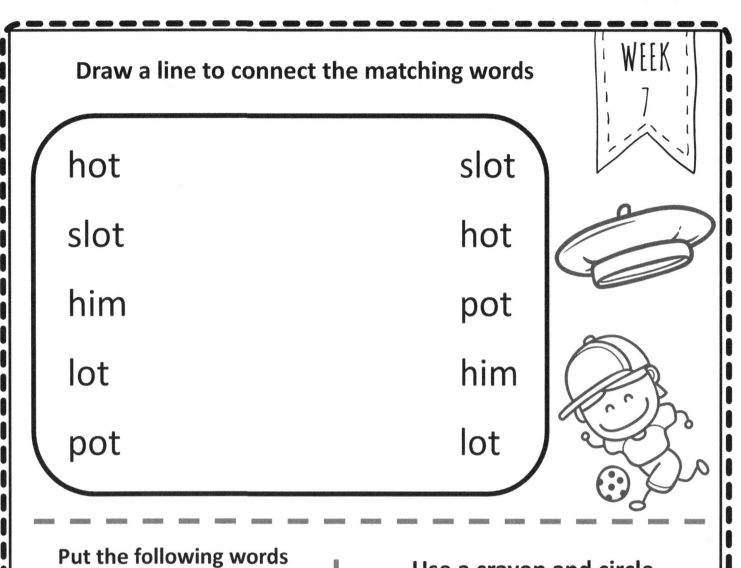

hot	slot
slot	hot
him	pot
lot	him
pot	lot

Put the following words in their correct shape boxes

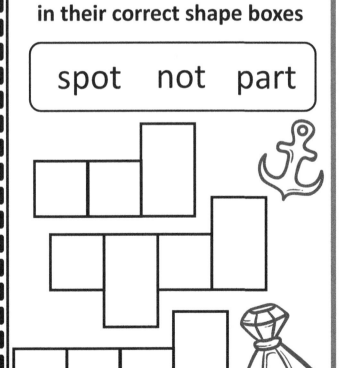

spot   not   part

Use a crayon and circle the spelling words below

drip	star	icon	leg
fly	dot	her	not
spot	bird	slot	next
key	nine	hot	run
blue	walk	we	sun
pot	you	dot	them

SPELLING WORDS

1. but
2. cut
3. grand
4. stand
5. land
6. band
7. and
8. do
9. shut
10. nut

Trace the word on the left,
then write it two more times on the right.

Use the below letters to complete the word.

d   a   s   g

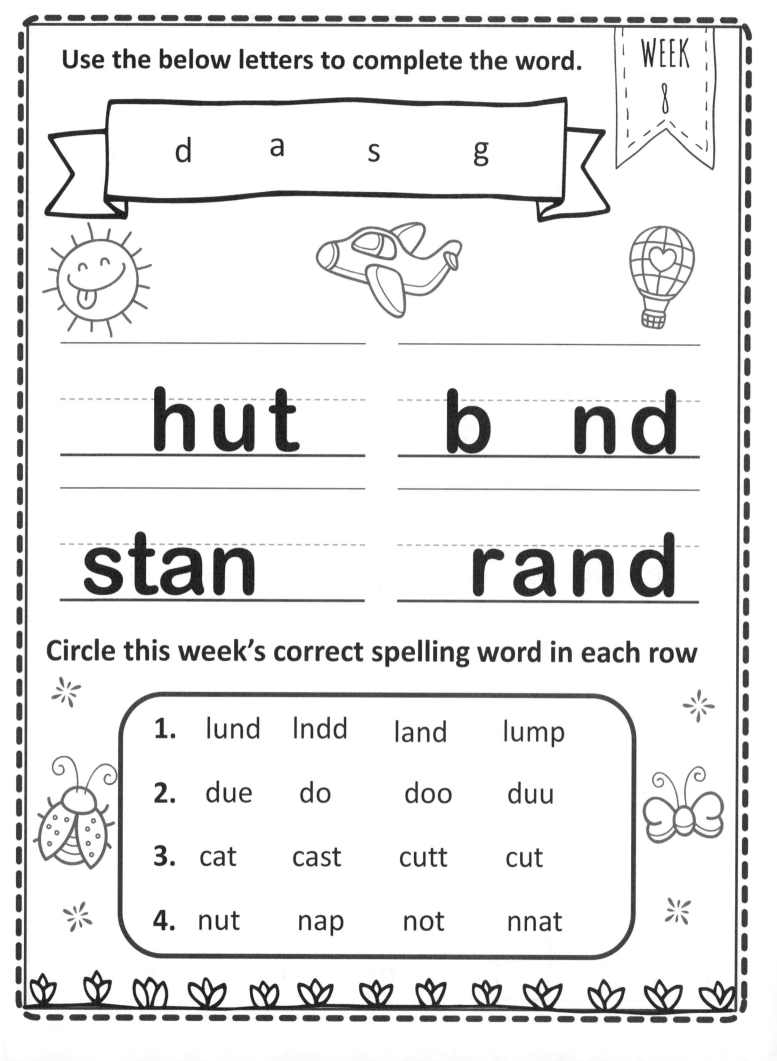

hut

b _ nd

stan

rand

Circle this week's correct spelling word in each row

1. lund   lndd   land   lump

2. due   do   doo   duu

3. cat   cast   cutt   cut

4. nut   nap   not   nnat

Draw a line to connect the matching words

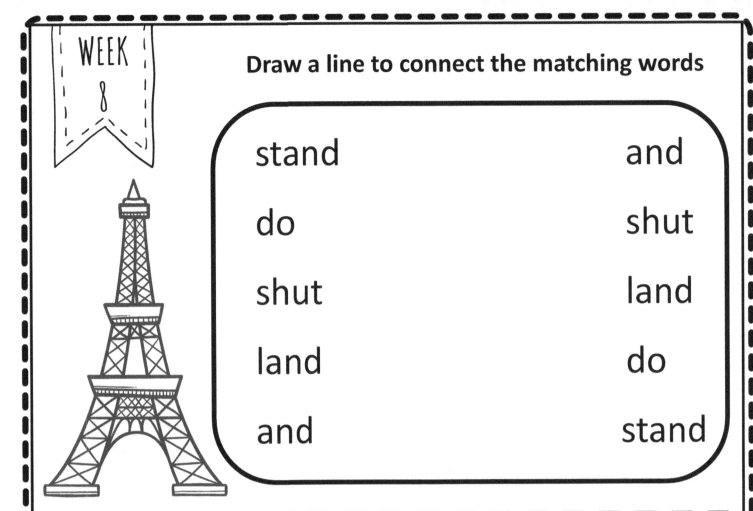

stand	and
do	shut
shut	land
land	do
and	stand

Put the following words in their correct shape boxes

band grand and

Circle and connect the spelling words to help the bee get to the bottom

rock	land	dirt	cut
fly	dot	band	help
rock	out	and	down
stand	nut	grass	do
fence	pear	shut	how
near	but	grand	fly

Find each of the spelling words in the word search below

STAND
GRAND
LAND
BAND
AND
DO
NUT
SHUT
BUT
CUT

T	V	V	Q	K	Q	F	I	V	A
B	A	N	D	V	C	Y	M	V	D
N	U	C	S	C	W	Z	T	N	R
K	U	U	H	H	C	M	A	B	K
P	X	T	O	G	U	L	G	N	K
W	D	O	O	B	U	T	R	O	D
C	L	S	T	A	N	D	A	G	H
N	X	P	C	P	R	F	N	C	I
R	D	H	G	P	D	G	D	D	X
U	A	X	P	C	B	L	E	R	M

Choose four words from the spelling list and write them below. Color each letter of the word with a different color.

_____   _____

_____   _____

WEEK 9

SPELLING WORDS

Trace the word on the left,
then write it two more times on the right.

1. can
2. fan
3. with
4. van
5. than
6. tan
7. ran
8. plan
9. pan
10. man

Find each of the spelling words in the word search below

I	R	F	C	D	T	L	K	K	I
N	A	U	A	H	F	Z	C	B	D
L	N	N	N	H	T	Z	X	F	E
N	W	A	V	P	L	A	N	G	L
V	T	J	H	Q	R	A	T	H	O
L	S	V	A	N	M	E	T	E	N
S	E	J	Y	V	H	I	H	X	U
O	W	W	D	E	W	P	A	N	N
G	Y	A	S	J	U	B	N	A	R
J	K	A	E	K	F	S	F	J	N

WITH

CAN

FAN

MAN

VAN

THAN

TAN

RAN

PLAN

PAN

Under each picture write the correct spelling of each word

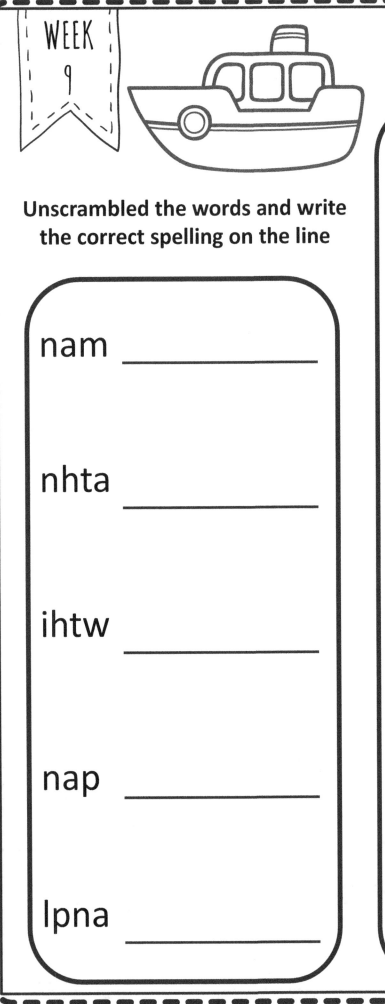

WEEK 9

Unscrambled the words and write the correct spelling on the line

nam _____

nhta _____

ihtw _____

nap _____

lpna _____

Put all of the spelling words in alphabetical order

1. _____

2. _____

3. _____

4. _____

5. _____

6. _____

7. _____

8. _____

9. _____

10. _____

Circle all of the letters in each spelling word

with	a w n d i u p o t v h
can	z t x c r u a j i n b l
plan	p s l d c u a o t e n
fan	a d n w v u g y f v j
than	a z m d t u i n r k h

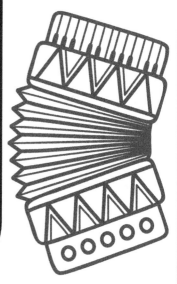

Put the following words in their correct shape boxes

with   ran   pan

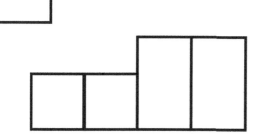

Color in each box that correctly spells your spelling words.

rn	fan	thane	mane	pan	plin
wite	dirt	plan	wuth	fon	wif
sky	tun	man	ron	thun	with
cana	mine	than	tan	tin	vane
pun	fin	ran	mun	thine	plat
van	tun	ven	pin	can	min

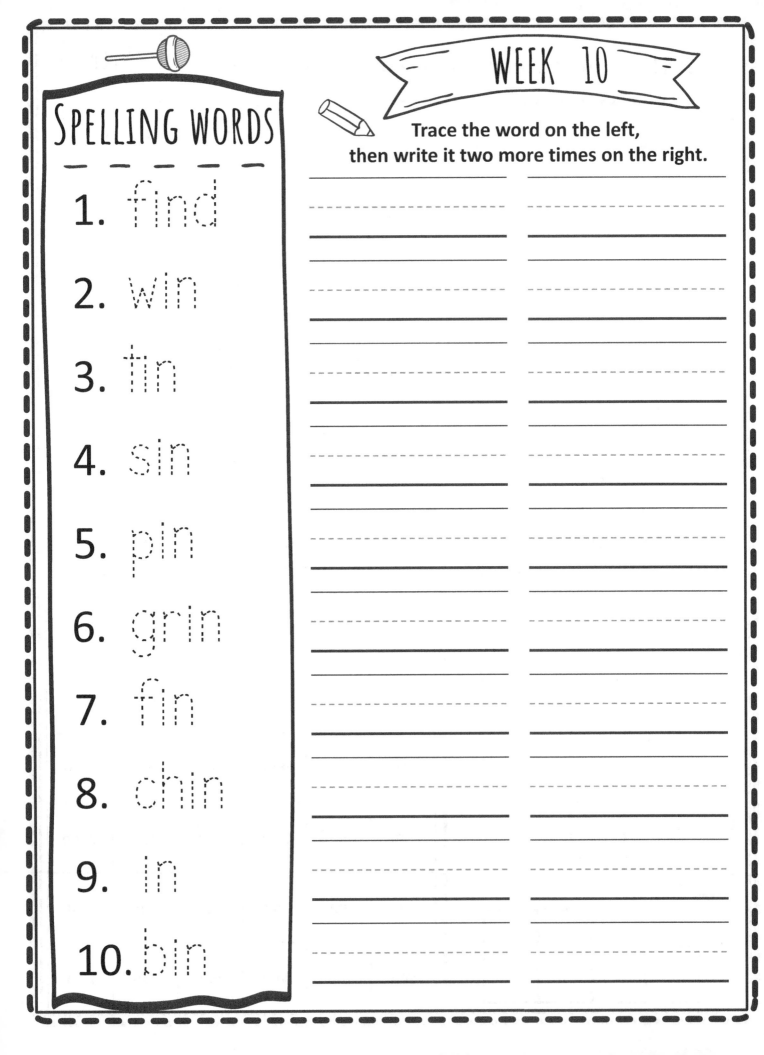

SPELLING WORDS

1. find
2. win
3. tin
4. sin
5. pin
6. grin
7. fin
8. chin
9. in
10. bin

Trace the word on the left,
then write it two more times on the right.

Write a spelling word in each of the kites.

WEEK 10

Find each of the spelling words in the word search below

U	D	M	H	A	C	U	G	Q	Z
N	L	P	M	V	B	B	R	S	W
O	F	S	D	I	W	I	I	I	X
T	I	X	O	P	I	F	N	N	T
G	N	J	V	W	I	I	X	L	I
S	H	N	D	N	F	N	N	Q	U
F	I	W	I	N	I	D	N	E	O
M	K	H	X	T	I	Q	N	A	D
T	C	I	W	G	B	M	Z	Q	W
B	G	A	P	Y	K	U	F	F	J

FIND
IN
WIN
BIN
CHIN
GRIN
SIN
TIN
PIN
FIN

Draw a line to connect the matching words

grin   pin

tin   tin

win   grin

find   win

pin   find

Use the words below to complete the sentences.

win

bin

find

tin

I hope we _____ .

It is made of _____ .

Did you _____ it?

Trash goes in the _____ .

SPELLING WORDS

1. or
2. more
3. out
4. have
5. our
6. has
7. was
8. are
9. about
10. for

**Trace the word on the left,
then write it two more times on the right.**

WEEK 11

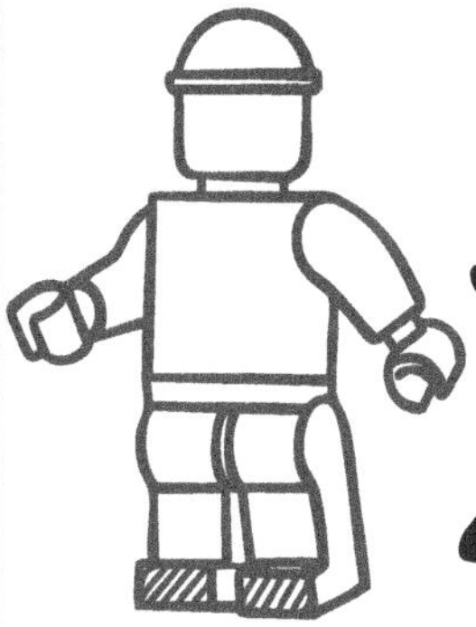

Use the below letters to complete the word.

u m v r

abo_t ____ _ore

ou_ ha_e

Circle this week's correct spelling word in each row

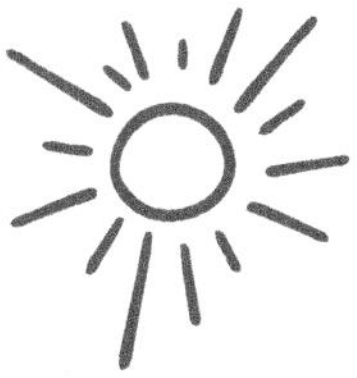

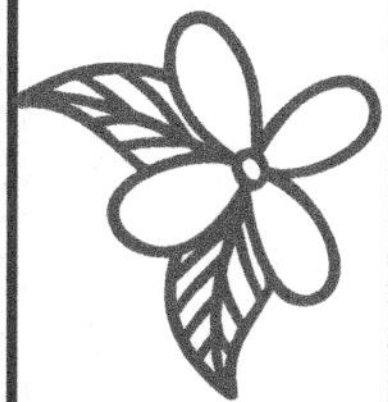

1.	aboot	abut	about	abbut
2.	mure	mire	doo	more
3.	ure	arre	aree	are
4.	was	wuz	waz	wuzz

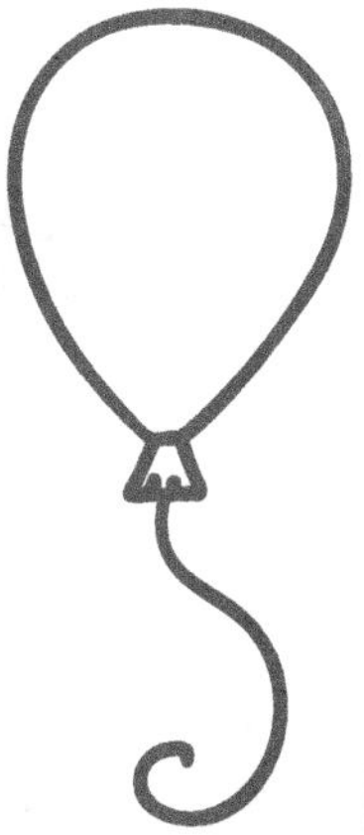

WEEK 11

Put all of the spelling words in alphabetical order

1. _____
2. _____
3. _____
4. _____
5. _____
6. _____
7. _____
8. _____
9. _____
10. _____

Unscrambled the words and write the correct spelling on the line

rof _____

aws _____

tuo _____

vahe _____

rea _____

Find each of the spelling words in the word search below

OUT									
ARE									
ABOUT									
MORE									
OR									
HAVE									
WAS									
OUR									
FOR									
HAS									

S	Y	W	A	H	M	M	Q	Z	G
G	G	C	N	C	A	R	P	N	M
J	L	L	R	Z	T	S	R	U	F
W	X	O	O	U	R	H	A	V	E
M	M	A	B	O	U	T	A	V	T
T	O	C	J	L	L	W	S	R	U
Y	R	U	B	E	Z	A	O	B	E
X	E	P	S	A	W	U	U	V	V
Z	D	O	E	A	D	W	T	L	X
H	I	R	K	F	O	R	Z	Z	X

Choose four words from the spelling list and write them below. Color each letter of the word with a different color.

_____   _____

_____   _____

SPELLING WORDS

Trace the word on the left,
then write it two more times on the right.

1. one
2. come
3. words
4. write
5. many
6. number
7. too
8. to
9. two
10. some

Read each sentence and circle the correct spelling word.

1. What is your favorite _____?   namber, number, numbur

2. How _____ kittens are there?   meny, manny, many, miny

3. Please _____ your name here.   wrute, wrate, write, wryte

4. Can I have _____ too?   some, sum, sime, suhm

Find each of the spelling words in the word search below

ONE		T	E	T	E	H	O	O	P	Z	F
COME		I	N	W	S	Q	P	T	B	U	L
WORDS		V	O	O	D	J	O	B	V	I	M
WRITE		L	R	T	R	O	X	E	F	Y	D
MANY		V	I	H	O	D	M	D	I	F	R
NUMBER		E	Z	F	W	O	K	Y	J	Q	E
TOO		N	T	E	S	B	E	I	F	M	B
TO		V	V	I	M	O	O	B	Y	A	M
TWO		F	G	H	R	O	W	W	K	N	U
SOME		Y	P	W	Z	W	C	M	Y	Y	N

Write each of the spelling words in the fish below

Put all of the spelling words in alphabetical order

1. _____
2. _____
3. _____
4. _____
5. _____
6. _____
7. _____
8. _____
9. _____
10. _____

Unscrambled the words and write the correct spelling on the line

myan   _____

odrsw   _____

treiw   _____

Write the correct spelling under each number below

1

_____

2

SPELLING WORDS

1. bad
2. dad
3. had
4. mad
5. pad
6. sad
7. tad
8. glad
9. add
10. into

WEEK 13

Trace the word on the left,
then write it two more times on the right.

Circle all of the letters in each spelling word

into	b e n x i f a c t o q
tad	e d z v a y b d i n t
glad	p l t d c g a o t a j k
add	g d n i a u g d f s e
mad	s z m s d f a n r m h

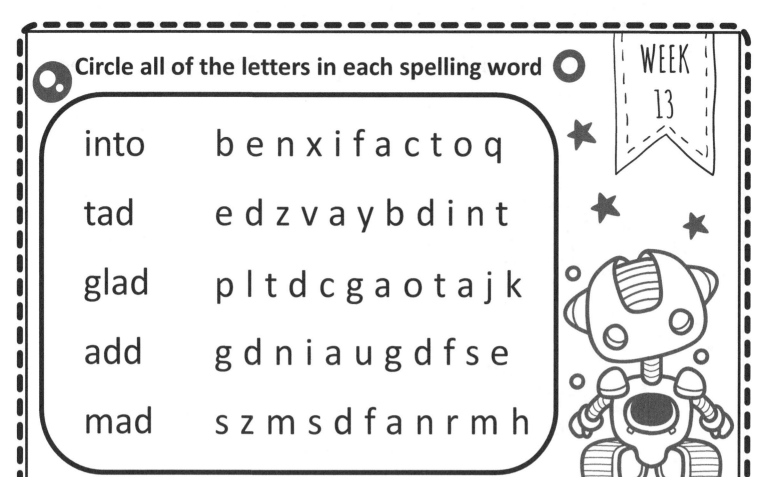

Put the following words in their correct shape boxes

into   pad   bad

Color in each box that correctly spells your spelling words.

dad	dade	tad	had	pan	add
sad	dirt	plan	wuth	aad	wif
sadd	tun	ppad	add	thun	glad
ada	pad	than	tan	mad	ssad
pun	haad	glaad	mun	thine	plat
into	tun	iinto	dadd	mude	bad

Write a spelling word in each of the puzzle pieces.

Find each of the spelling words in the word search below

F	T	Y	Y	W	F	O	J	I	D
H	A	D	S	G	F	B	U	S	A
T	H	T	R	W	U	D	S	L	D
Z	S	A	D	S	P	A	D	S	Y
Q	P	D	L	J	F	U	B	Y	A
M	Z	H	Z	N	U	R	D	F	P
H	P	X	Q	D	R	A	E	P	X
G	D	B	H	B	B	Y	M	L	Q
K	D	W	S	A	Z	G	L	A	D
L	A	D	I	N	T	O	P	N	D

BAD

INTO

DAD

GLAD

ADD

HAD

SAD

PAD

TAD

MAD

Use the below letters to complete each word.

d   i   m   l   n

g _ ad

_ to

da _

_ ad

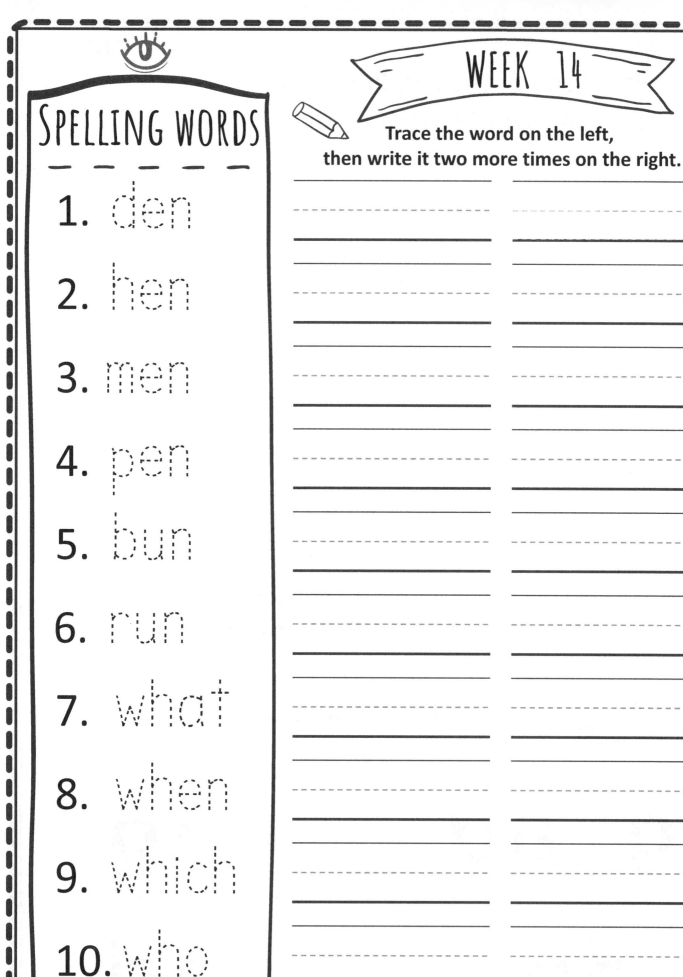

SPELLING WORDS

WEEK 14

Trace the word on the left,
then write it two more times on the right.

1. den
2. hen
3. men
4. pen
5. bun
6. run
7. what
8. when
9. which
10. who

WEEK 14

Use different colors to fill in each of the spelling word letters.

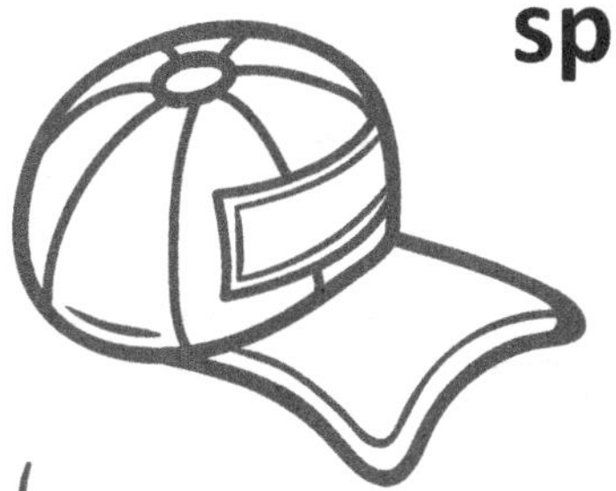

who

den

hen

which

run

bun

pen

men

When

what

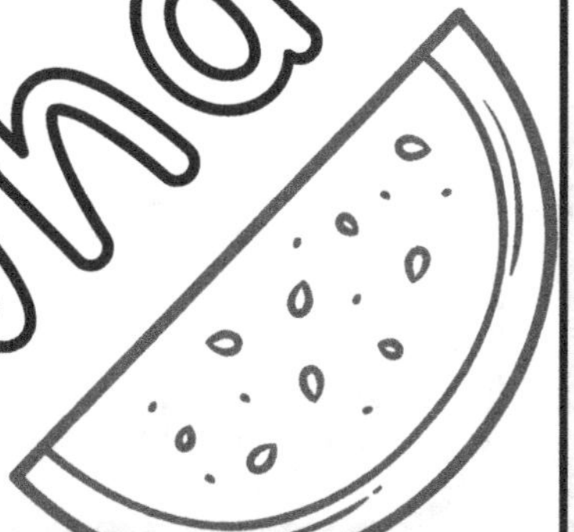

Use the words below to complete the sentences.

pen   when   run   who

Write with
a _____ .

I like to
_____ .

_____ are
they?

_____ does
it start ?

Circle this week's correct spelling word in each row

1. heen   hene   hen   henn

2. whhic   which   wich   whicch

3. whu   whoo   woo   who

4. bun   buun   bbn   bunn

Put all of the spelling words in alphabetical order

1. _____
2. _____
3. _____
4. _____
5. _____
6. _____
7. _____
8. _____
9. _____
10. _____

WEEK 14

Unscrambled the words and write the correct spelling on the line

hwihc _____

urn _____

epn _____

nub _____

ned _____

henw _____

tahw _____

SPELLING WORDS

Trace the word on the left, then write it two more times on the right.

1. block

2. bed

3. red

4. fed

5. yes

6. shed

7. sled

8. led

9. rod

10. pillow

Find each of the spelling words in the word search below

N	R	E	D	D	Q	B	X	S	P
A	Y	E	E	P	Q	L	B	E	W
R	E	L	E	D	I	O	G	E	W
E	S	X	O	F	R	C	A	D	D
X	K	S	I	E	O	K	W	B	Z
M	S	A	R	D	D	O	V	P	U
G	H	C	F	U	L	C	A	S	Y
O	E	B	V	L	A	W	F	X	Z
L	D	D	I	R	A	V	Q	V	L
C	O	P	Z	Q	K	O	X	T	X

PILLOW

BED

FED

RED

SHED

SLED

BLOCK

YES

ROD

LED

Under each picture write the correct spelling of each word

_____

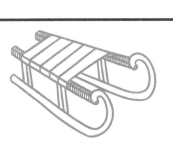

_____   _____

Write each of the spelling words in the lily pads below

Draw a line to connect the matching words

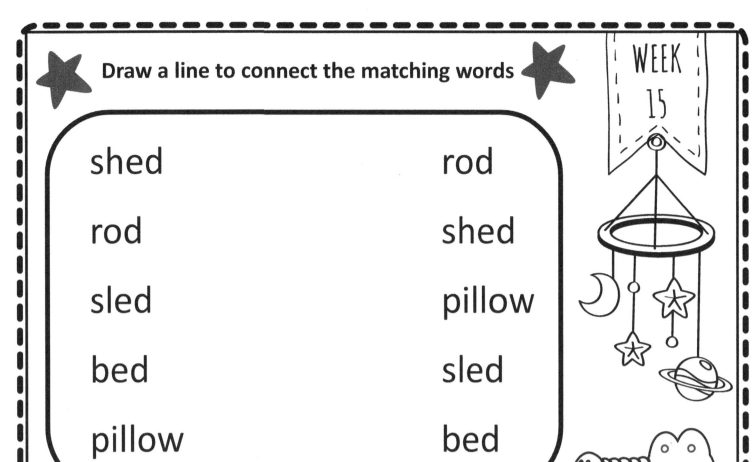

shed	rod
rod	shed
sled	pillow
bed	sled
pillow	bed

Put the following words in their correct shape boxes

sled   yes   red

Use a crayon and circle the spelling words below

fed	sled	let	bed
fly	stripe	no	led
shed	block	slot	rod
hole	nine	red	run
yes	walk	we	tip
green	us	pillow	sick

SPELLING WORDS

1. snob
2. side
3. sob
4. did
5. hid
6. kid
7. lid
8. rid
9. mob
10. job

Trace the word on the left,
then write it two more times on the right.

Put all of the spelling words in alphabetical order

1. _____
2. _____
3. _____
4. _____
5. _____
6. _____
7. _____
8. _____
9. _____
10. _____

WEEK 16

Unscrambled the words and write the correct spelling on the line

obj _____

dsie _____

dki _____

Put the following words in their correct shape boxes

snob   lid   hid

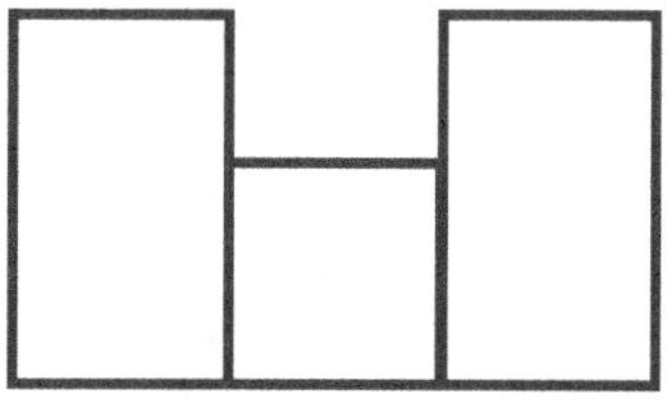

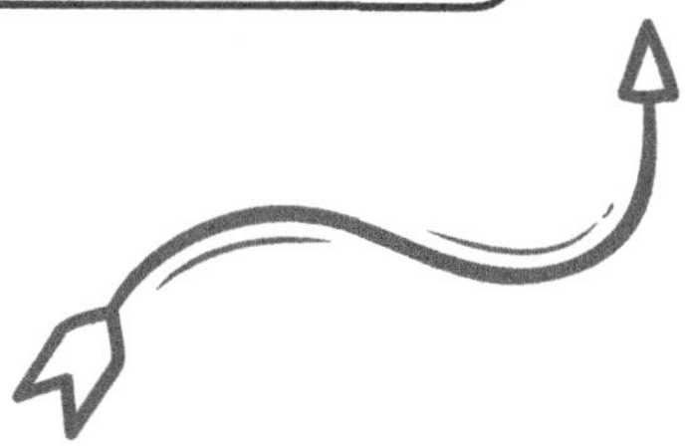

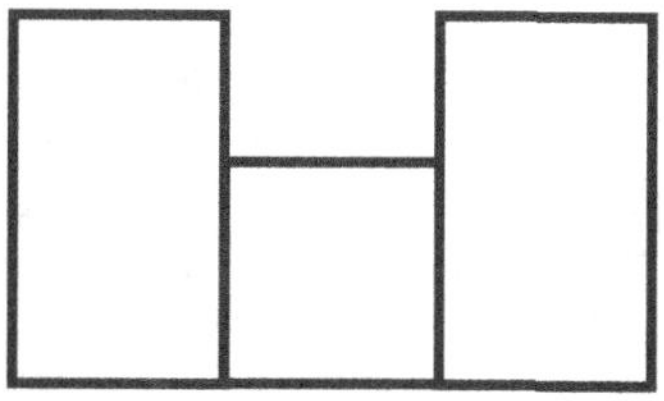

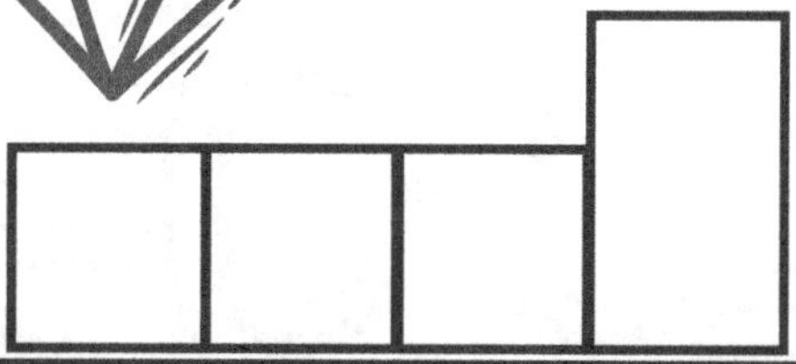

Help the robot write a different spelling word on each step on the ladder.

Find each of the spelling words in the word search below

M	O	B	D	K	H	A	R	K	A
A	O	J	D	N	I	J	D	M	U
S	E	D	O	C	D	D	C	L	O
L	R	X	D	B	Q	V	U	M	D
I	C	I	B	F	Y	U	R	L	Q
G	L	O	R	I	G	V	T	E	C
K	N	S	I	D	E	C	C	Z	L
S	K	F	D	D	J	H	A	O	M
M	M	F	I	Q	R	Y	D	I	J
J	N	D	X	Y	M	W	V	F	T

DID

HID

KID

LID

RID

MOB

SOB

SIDE

SNOB

JOB

Circle this week's correct spelling word in each row

1. liid   lid   lud   lide

2. mab   moob   mob   mobb

3. side   syde   sighed   seyed

4. rud   ridd   riid   rid

SPELLING WORDS

Trace the word on the left,
then write it two more times on the right.

1. tub

2. cab

3. rub

4. lab

5. crab

6. cub

7. rib

8. scab

9. bib

10. web

Find each of the spelling words in the word search below

WEEK 17

A	J	E	N	N	M	U	O	U	B
R	C	P	W	I	V	V	Y	R	I	I
C	C	L	Q	A	X	J	B	B	I
R	R	C	A	B	Q	L	L	D	H
A	T	S	X	B	O	K	R	U	B
B	M	K	C	M	W	E	B	R	T
A	D	E	U	J	R	A	R	U	U
I	Q	L	B	O	I	L	F	Q	B
E	B	S	C	A	B	P	P	G	C
G	Y	Q	N	A	C	U	C	V	M

TUB
RUB
CAB
LAB
CUB
RIB
BIB
CRAB
SCAB
WEB

Under each picture write the correct spelling of each word

_____

_____

WEEK 17

Teddy loves to read.

Help him write spelling words on each book and then color them!

Put all of the spelling words in alphabetical order

1. _____
2. _____
3. _____
4. _____
5. _____
6. _____
7. _____
8. _____
9. _____
10. _____

Read each sentence and circle the correct spelling word.

1. A spider makes a _____.   webb, weeb, web, weebb

2. Look at that cute baby _____ !   cab, cub, cuub, cubb, ccub

3. The water is warm in the _____. tabb, tube, tub, tuhb

4. Don't scratch your _____.   skab, scahb, scab, skabb

5. Don't let the _____ pinch you.   krab, chrab, crab, crrab

Put the following words in their correct shape boxes

tub   web   crab

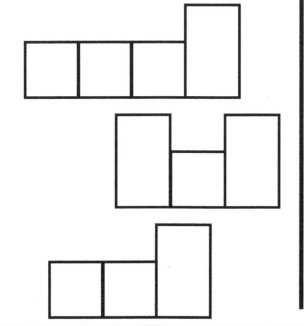

Color in each box that correctly spells your spelling words.

rb	ribe	ruub	ttub	cabb	sad
wite	tub	plan	wuth	cab	wif
sky	tun	rub	lab	labe	with
cana	biib	crab	cub	tin	vane
wweb	scab	ran	mun	rib	weeb
web	top	down	ccab	lab	bib

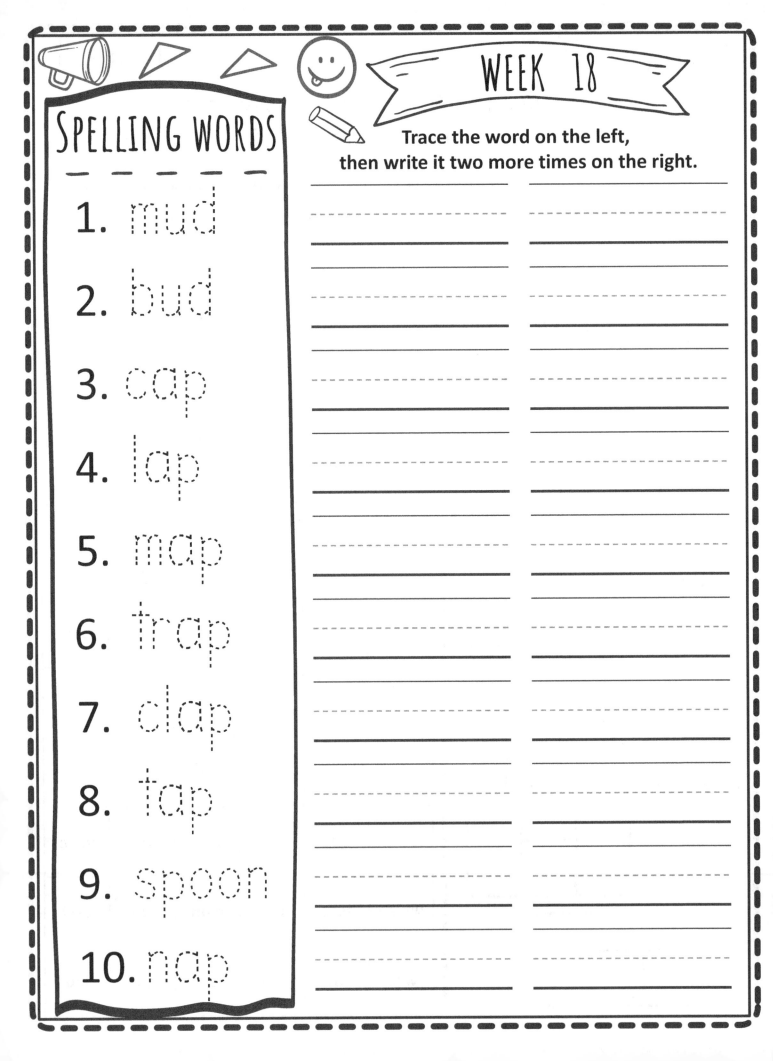

SPELLING WORDS

1. mud
2. bud
3. cap
4. lap
5. map
6. trap
7. clap
8. tap
9. spoon
10. nap

Trace the word on the left,
then write it two more times on the right.

Find each of the spelling words in the word search below

WEEK 18

A	I	T	A	P	R	H	R	T	H
N	F	F	B	W	Y	Q	J	V	U
H	O	L	A	N	Y	W	G	M	U
U	B	N	O	B	O	S	H	X	U
N	A	O	B	D	R	D	V	B	H
E	P	O	U	T	C	L	E	P	X
S	I	S	D	M	C	A	A	L	N
Y	Z	X	M	U	A	L	P	N	F
N	E	F	U	Z	C	P	A	A	K
N	M	H	D	J	T	R	A	P	Y

MUD

BUD

TRAP

CLAP

TAP

SPOON

MAP

CAP

NAP

LAP

Circle this week's correct spelling word in each row

1. spuun   spune   spon   spoon

2. trap   trape   trapp   traap

3. buud   bud   buhd   budd

4. myp   mup   map   maap

WEEK 18

Help the eggs hatch by writing your spelling words on each of them. Then have fun coloring!

Draw a line to connect the matching words

bud	clap
clap	bud
map	spoon
trap	map
spoon	trap

Use the words below to complete the sentences.

nap   map   tap   mud

Don't step in the _____ .

I can read a _____ .

Don't _____ the glass.

I need a _____ .

SPELLING WORDS

1. drip
2. dip
3. flip
4. hip
5. chip
6. lip
7. rip
8. zip
9. tip
10. sip

Trace the word on the left,
then write it two more times on the right.

Find each of the spelling words in the word search below

J	G	F	L	I	P	O	D	W	I
Y	H	P	H	U	J	N	A	S	W
T	I	N	F	L	D	H	I	S	I
Z	O	C	D	I	Y	R	I	I	T
Z	T	T	C	P	C	H	I	P	I
B	O	V	Y	D	O	V	J	P	P
A	W	G	B	D	J	R	P	U	U
V	G	D	P	F	I	S	X	A	G
X	I	I	Z	G	P	C	O	X	V
M	R	P	V	K	X	F	U	N	L

DRIP

FLIP

CHIP

ZIP

TIP

ZIP

SIP

RIP

LIP

HIP

Use the letters below to complete the word. Trace the full word.

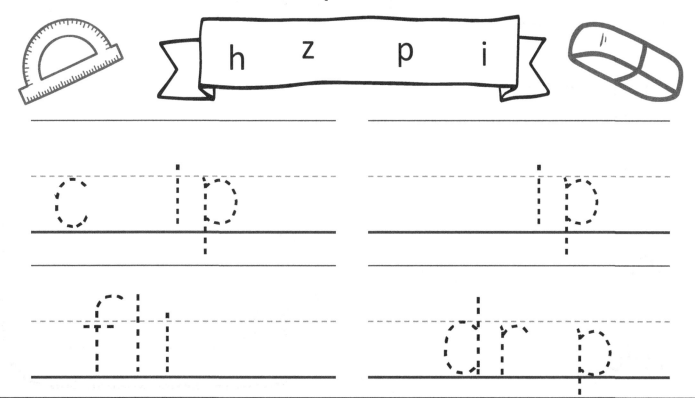

h   z   p   i

c _ i p

_ i p

f l i _

d r _ p

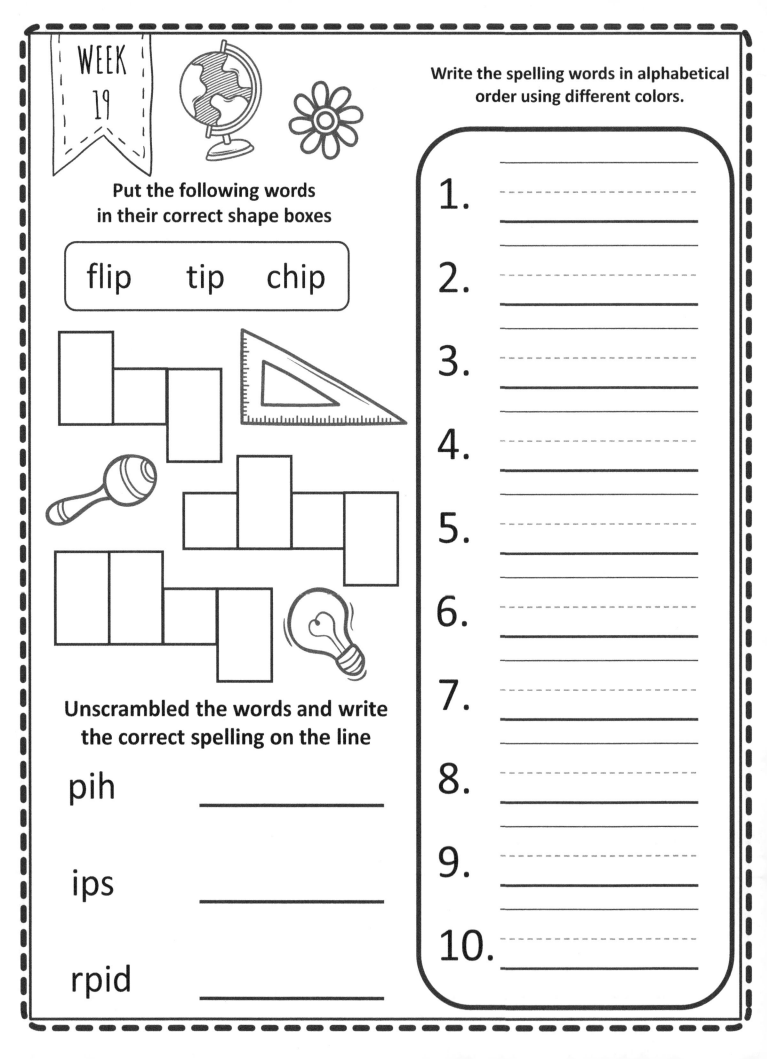

WEEK 19

Put the following words in their correct shape boxes

flip   tip   chip

Unscrambled the words and write the correct spelling on the line

pih _____

ips _____

rpid _____

Write the spelling words in alphabetical order using different colors.

1. _____
2. _____
3. _____
4. _____
5. _____
6. _____
7. _____
8. _____
9. _____
10. _____

Draw pictures of your favorite spelling words and then label them

Circle this week's correct spelling word in each row

Circle all of the letters in each spelling word

1. syp, siip, sup, sip

2. rup, ripe, rip, riip

3. llip, lip, lihp, lipp

4. hep, hyp, hiip, hip

5. dpp, dipp, dip, dyyp

drip	z e d x i f r p
flip	p d i v a l b f
chip	p l h e c g i p
zip	s p n i b z g r
tip	l z p s i f a t

SPELLING WORDS

Trace the word on the left,
then write it two more times on the right.

1. people

2. cop

3. hop

4. chop

5. flop

6. stop

7. use

8. top

9. pop

10. mop

Use the words below to complete the sentences.

use   chop   top   hop

Put the paper
on _____ .

_____ soap
to clean it.

Slowly _____
it with a knife .

I can _____
on one leg.

Circle this week's correct spelling word in each row

1. stap   stup   stop   stopp

2. mup   mop   mopp   mmop

3. peeple   peiple   pipl   people

4. cop   capp   cuup   cahp

Help the puppy find his home.
Write a spelling word in each bone.

Put the following words
in their correct shape boxes

pop   use   flop

Find each of the spelling words in the word search below

| PEOPLE |
| USE |
| STOP |
| FLOP |
| CHOP |
| TOP |
| POP |
| MOP |
| HOP |
| COP |

Y	S	C	H	G	L	T	A	A	U
Z	A	O	O	T	W	P	O	P	R
I	Z	P	S	X	H	E	E	P	W
L	S	K	S	P	L	F	D	C	E
A	S	T	O	P	Z	F	V	D	Q
A	C	H	O	P	Z	L	L	S	L
C	F	E	M	P	J	S	C	O	J
O	P	O	O	D	T	U	S	E	P
J	C	B	P	U	C	K	N	B	U
J	H	W	F	U	L	V	Q	O	I

Read each sentence and circle the correct spelling word.

1. Please _____ running inside.   stap, stup, stop, stahp

2. How many _____ are there?   pepl, peepl, people, pepul

3. I like to drink _____.   pup, pahp, pop, ppop

4. The _____ makes me feel safe.   cap, cop, coop, cahp, caap

SPELLING WORDS

Trace the word on the left,
then write it two more times on the right.

1. first

2. cup

3. flag

4. pup

5. brag

6. each

7. tag

8. bag

9. reach

10. rag

Put all of the spelling words in alphabetical order

Unscrambled the words and write the correct spelling on the line

rabg _____

irsft _____

upp _____

Put the following words in their correct shape boxes

reach   cup   each

1. _____

2. _____

3. _____

4. _____

5. _____

6. _____

7. _____

8. _____

9. _____

10. _____

Find each of the spelling words in the word search below

R	V	G	M	H	F	V	L	C	L
R	P	P	G	N	I	C	Z	H	Z
M	U	F	R	G	R	J	U	R	L
C	P	Z	F	S	S	E	R	K	E
D	B	A	C	L	T	I	A	N	A
A	B	R	J	T	A	G	G	C	C
S	S	N	A	Z	A	G	D	P	H
I	B	O	A	G	E	I	C	F	Q
B	A	J	U	W	O	O	M	O	B
L	G	I	W	S	S	U	S	V	S

FIRST

PUP

FLAG

CUP

EACH

REACH

BAG

RAG

TAG

BRAG

Under each picture write the correct spelling of each word

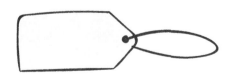

WEEK 22

SPELLING WORDS

1. other
2. beg
3. water
4. leg
5. wig
6. peg
7. pig
8. fig
9. dig
10. big

Trace the word on the left,
then write it two more times on the right.

Find each of the spelling words in the word search below

E	C	R	C	E	D	Z	F	I	G
V	K	P	B	E	G	W	F	R	F
A	B	I	Z	G	P	E	R	Y	C
W	I	G	E	S	I	E	D	H	O
Q	V	L	X	P	T	Z	G	Y	T
D	W	T	B	A	F	J	V	Z	H
I	O	S	W	I	G	E	B	C	E
G	P	G	N	W	G	R	A	G	R
C	Z	Y	C	G	S	A	E	T	H
Q	B	W	U	A	G	Q	F	F	A

WATER

BEG

OTHER

WIG

LEG

PEG

BIG

DIG

FIG

PIG

Use the letters below to complete the word. Trace the full word.

W   o   e   i

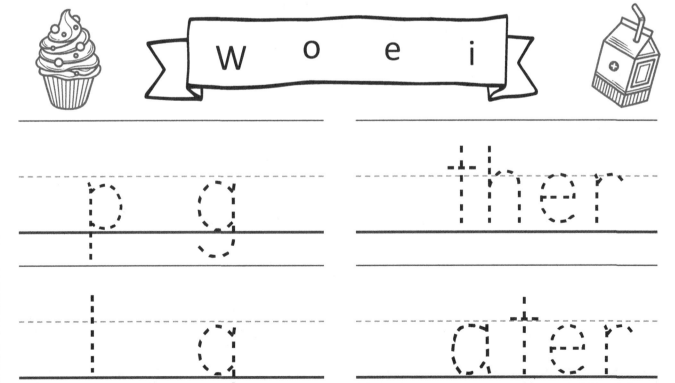

p _ g

_ther

_ _ g

_ater

Label each jar with a different spelling word.
Then color each one!

Draw a line to connect the matching words

dig   big

big   dig

wig   other

fig   wig

other   fig

Put the following words in their correct shape boxes

water leg wig

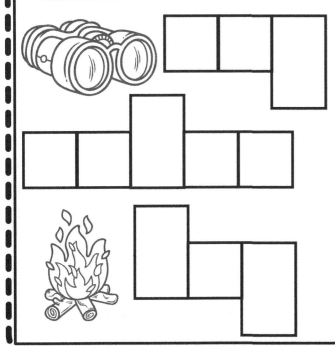

 **Use a crayon and circle the spelling words below**

apple	other	jet	snap
water	peg	wig	big
fig	dig	pig	wow
red	leg	lip	set
yes	walk	beg	up
key	other	sock	top

SPELLING WORDS

Trace the word on the left,
then write it two more times on the right.

1. were

2. rug

3. mug

4. dog

5. jog

6. fog

7. log

8. dug

9. hug

10. jug

Find each of the spelling words in the word search below

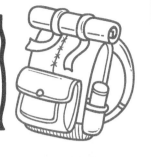

U	R	K	Y	V	X	N	I	E	F
D	U	T	U	A	Q	Q	Y	Q	J
K	V	J	U	G	L	B	Y	M	F
M	N	D	O	Z	B	D	R	A	J
U	G	L	R	M	Q	T	H	G	V
G	D	W	E	R	E	D	U	G	F
J	O	G	C	I	D	R	G	K	O
I	O	R	B	Z	O	T	Q	R	S
F	Q	E	V	K	G	P	E	J	K
G	V	Z	F	X	E	X	O	E	Y

DUG

HUG

JUG

MUG

RUG

WERE

DOG

FOG

JOG

LOG

Draw four of your favorite spelling words.
Under each picture write the correct spelling of each word.

_____   _____

_____   _____

Put all of the spelling words in alphabetical order

Unscrambled the words and write the correct spelling on the line

eerw _____

urg _____

goj _____

odg _____

guh _____

gud _____

olg _____

1. _____

2. _____

3. _____

4. _____

5. _____

6. _____

7. _____

8. _____

9. _____

10. _____

Help the campers see the stars. Write a spelling word on each star. Then have fun coloring!

WEEK 23

SPELLING WORDS

1. long
2. called
3. small
4. wall
5. tall
6. all
7. fall
8. call
9. ball
10. hall

Trace the word on the left,
then write it two more times on the right.

Rex the dinosaur is going on a road trip! He's going to be VERY hungry. Help write the spelling words on each of the sandwiches.

WEEK 24

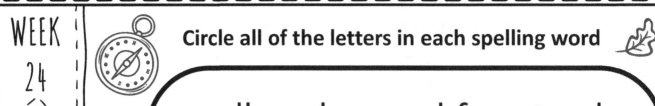

WEEK 24

Circle all of the letters in each spelling word

wall	b a n x l f a c t w l
long	o d z l a y b g i n v
small	p l t m c l a o t s j q
ball	l d b i a u g d f l e
called	a d c s l p a e r l h

Put the following words in their correct shape boxes

small   all   fall

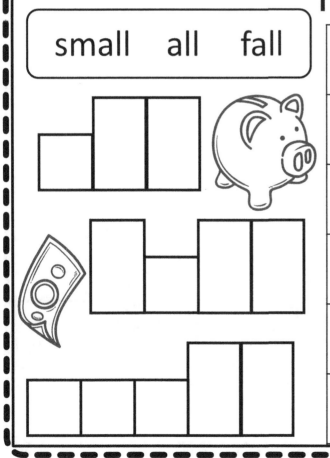

Shade in each box that correctly spells this week's spelling words.

long	dade	tad	call	fal	add
sad	called	longe	wuth	fall	all
sadd	bal	small	add	bball	hall
ada	fad	wall	tan	alle	ssad
wale	haad	sta	mun	tall	plat
cal	tun	wwal	dadd	calle	ball

Put all of the spelling words in alphabetical order

1. _____
2. _____
3. _____
4. _____
5. _____
6. _____
7. _____
8. _____
9. _____
10. _____

Unscrambled the words and write the correct spelling on the line

olng _____

lawl _____

altl _____

llaced _____

lla _____

MORE WRITING PRACTICE!

Choose any of your favorite spelling words and write them below at least five times each.

1.

2.

3.

4.

5.

6.

7.

8.

9.

10.

Answer Key

Scholastic Panda Education

We 🤍 trees, which is why we've made the answer key digital.

Visit the below link to easily download it:

https://bit.ly/3PUTp7C

Bonus

Leave this book a review and
we may send you something special.